Fact Finders™

Great Inventions

THE BICYCLE

by Larry Hills

Capstone
press

Mankato, Minnesota

Fact Finders is published by Capstone Press
151 Good Counsel Drive, P.O. Box 669, Mankato, Minnesota 56002
www.capstonepress.com

Library of Congress Cataloging-in-Publication Data
Hills, Larry.
    The bicycle/by Larry Hills.
      p. cm.—(Fact finders. Great inventions)
    Includes bibliographical references and index.
    ISBN 0-7368-2668-8 (hardcover)
    1. Bicycles—History—Juvenile literature. [1. Bicycles and bicycling—History.
2. Inventions.] I. Title. II. Series.
TL412.H55 2004
629.227'2—dc22   2003026783

Summary: Introduces the history and development of the bicycle and explains how
    a bicycle works.

Editorial Credits
Christopher Harbo, editor; Juliette Peters, series designer; Patrick Dentinger, book designer
    and illustrator; Kelly Garvin, photo researcher; Eric Kudalis, product planning editor

Photo Credits
Capstone Press/Gary Sundermeyer, cover, 1, 27 (all)
Corbis/Bettmann, 8, 26 (left and right); Brooks Craft, 13; Hulton-Deutsch Collection, 6–7,
    12, 16, 26 (middle); Owen Franken, 9
Getty Images Inc./Hulton Archive, 14–15, 18; Robert Laberge, 4–5; Ryan Pierse, 21
Mary Evans Picture Library, 17
Richard L. Miller, 19
Stock Montage Inc., 11
Transworld BMX/Keith Mulligan, 24–25
UNICORN Stock Photos/Susan McGee, 23

**Fact Finders thanks Roger White of the Transportation Collections at the Smithsonian
Institution, Washington, D.C., for reviewing this book.**

1 2 3 4 5 6 09 08 07 06 05 04

Table of Contents

Chapter 1

Tour de France

The Tour de France is the most famous bicycle race in the world. It runs more than 2,000 miles (3,200 kilometers) through France.

In 2003, people around the world watched American cyclist Lance Armstrong. He had won the Tour de France every year since 1999. If he won again, Armstrong would be the second person to win five years in a row.

On the last day of the race, Armstrong had a slim lead. Jan Ullrich of Germany was about one minute behind. Ullrich gained time, but he could not catch up. Armstrong rode a strong race. He won his fifth straight Tour de France.

Lance Armstrong, wearing a yellow jersey, rounds a corner during the 2003 Tour de France.

The bicycles that Armstrong and other modern cyclists ride are built for racing. These bicycles are designed to be light and fast. They are the result of nearly 200 years of changes to bicycle designs.

Chapter 2

Before the Bicycle

People traveled in many ways before the bicycle was invented. For thousands of years, people walked or rode animals to move from place to place. When the wheel was invented, people built new ways to travel. The cart, the chariot, the wagon, and the carriage all used wheels. Usually, these inventions were pulled by animals.

F A C T !

Many scientists believe the wheel was invented about 5,000 years ago in Mesopotamia. This area lies in southwest Asia.

Before the bicycle, animals helped people travel. Mail carriers used horses and buggies to deliver mail.

Leonardo da Vinci's Drawings

More than 500 years ago, Leonardo da Vinci drew ideas for vehicles. Leonardo was a famous Italian artist and inventor. Some of his ideas were vehicles powered by people. One of his most famous sketches was of a flying machine. Leonardo's flying machine is similar to a modern-day helicopter.

Leonardo da Vinci drew an idea for a flying machine that looked like a helicopter. ▼

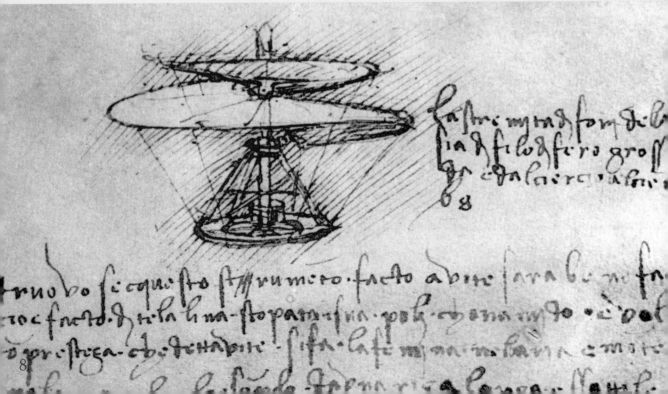

▲ A museum in Vinci, Italy, displays a model based on Leonardo da Vinci's drawing of a bicycle.

Leonardo also had ideas for land vehicles that people could power. Around 1490, he sketched a machine similar to the first bicycles. His machine had two wheels, a seat, and pedals.

Leonardo never built his machine. The world would have to wait more than 300 years for the first bicycle.

Chapter 3

Early Inventions

The bicycle was not invented by just one person. It was invented by several people over many years.

The First Bicycle

Many historians agree that the first bicycle was built in 1817. Baron Karl Drais Von Sauerbrun of Germany called his invention the *draisine*. It was also known as the hobby horse.

The *draisine* was made of wood. It was pushed forward by the rider's feet. It had two wooden wheels connected by a beam. A seat was in the middle of the beam. The rider steered with a handle fixed to the front wheel.

Riders pushed the *draisine* forward with their feet.

The First Pedals

In 1839, a Scottish blacksmith named
Kirkpatrick Macmillan made the first
bicycle pedals. He attached pedals to
swinging **cranks** above the bicycle's
front wheel. The swinging cranks were
linked to rods that drove the back wheel.
These parts made the bicycle too heavy
to ride very far.

▲ Kirkpatrick
Macmillan's
bicycle was
the first to
use pedals.

The Velocipede

In the 1860s, Frenchmen Pierre Michaux and Pierre Lallement both put pedals on velocipede bicycles. These bicycles had iron frames. Their wheels were made of iron and wood. Their pedals were attached to the front wheels.

The velocipede was heavy. It required strength to pedal and steer. The velocipede was very rough to ride. Some people called it the boneshaker.

FACT!

In the late 1860s, Sylvester H. Roper from Massachusetts built a steam-powered velocipede. A small steam engine powered the bicycle's back wheel.

The velocipede's pedals were connected to the front wheel.

Changes to the Bicycle

In the early 1800s, few people rode bicycles. But by the late 1800s, bicycles were a popular way to travel.

The Ordinary

In 1871, the first ordinary, or high wheel, bicycles were built. The ordinary had a large front wheel and a small back wheel. The pedals were attached to the front wheel. With each turn of the pedals, the rider could cover a lot of ground. The ordinary's seat was placed over the front wheel. This placement helped the rider push the pedals.

The Safety Bicycle

In 1885, John Starley of England built the first modern bicycle. The Starley Rover had two wheels that were close to the same size. It was driven by pedals on a large gear. The teeth on the gear gripped the links of a chain attached to the back wheel. As the rider pedaled, the gear drove the chain.

The Starley Rover did not tip over as easily as the ordinary. It became known as the safety bicycle.

The Starley Rover used a chain connected to gears on the ▼ back wheel.

THE ROVER SAFETY BICYCLE (PATENTED).

BRADLEY BIRM'S

Safer than any Tricycle, faster and easier than any Bicycle ever made. Fitted with handles to turn for convenience in storing or shipping. Far and away the best hill-climber in the market.

MANUFACTURED BY

STARLEY & SUTTON,

METEOR WORKS, WEST ORCHARD, COVENTRY, ENGLAND.

More Improvements

Bicycles changed in other ways in the 1870s and 1880s. Solid iron frames were replaced with hollow steel frames. Hollow frames made bicycles lighter and easier to control.

In 1888, John Boyd Dunlop from Ireland introduced air-filled bicycle tires. He made the tires so riders could enjoy a smoother bicycle ride.

John Boyd Dunlop stands beside a bicycle with air-filled tires.

Bicycles for Children

By the 1930s, companies were selling many bicycles for children. These bicycles had large tires, colorful frames, and chrome handlebars.

In the mid-1960s, the Schwinn Stingray was a popular bicycle for kids. The frames were painted bright colors. Stingrays had banana-shaped seats and high-rise handlebars.

The Schwinn Stingray was a very popular children's bike in the mid- to late 1960s.

Chapter 5

How Bicycles Work

Bicycles work by changing power from a rider's legs into forward motion. A rider pushes the pedals to turn cranks. The cranks turn the **chain wheel**. This gear moves a chain. The chain turns the **freewheel** on the back wheel. As this wheel turns, the bicycle moves forward.

Changing Gears

Most bicycles have a freewheel with several gears. Gears control how much the back wheel turns. A low gear uses several turns of the pedals to turn the back wheel once. A high gear uses one turn of the pedals to turn the back wheel several times.

Bicycle riders use gears to help them pedal up hills.

Bicycle riders change gears to make pedaling easier. Lower gears are easier to pedal on hills. On flat areas, riders use higher gears.

The rider changes gears by adjusting a gear lever. The gear lever moves the **derailleur** near the freewheel. A derailleur is a small arm that keeps tension on the chain. The derailleur also moves the chain up and down the gears on the freewheel.

Many parts work together to make a bicycle move ▼ forward.

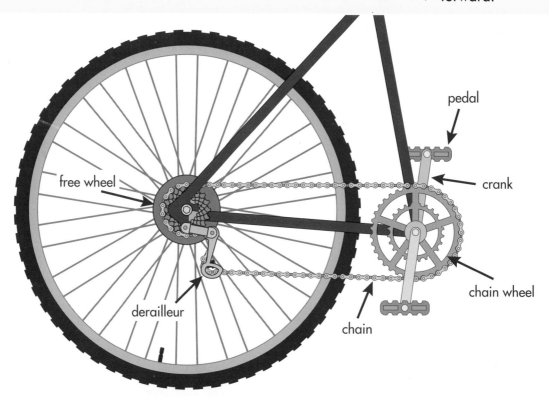

pedal

crank

chain wheel

free wheel

derailleur

chain

Brakes

Bicycles would be dangerous without good brakes. Most bicycles use **friction** braking. Brake levers on the·handlebars are connected to cables. The cables lead to **calipers** on the front and rear wheels. Calipers press rubber brake pads to the wheel rims. The friction makes the bicycle slow to a stop.

Some bicycles use **hydraulic** disc brakes. These brakes use fluids in tubes to press brake pads against the wheels.

▲ Rubber brake pads rub against the rim of the wheel to help slow down a bicycle.

Chapter 6

Bicycles Today

Over the years, bicycles have been built for many sports and activities. Road racing bikes are built for speed. They have light frames and thin tires. Off-road bikes are built to handle bumps and jumps. They have strong frames and thicker tires. Today, BMX and mountain bikes are two popular bicycle styles.

BMX Bikes

The first bicycle motocross, or BMX, bikes were built in the 1970s. They had small, strong frames and thick tires. They were built for racing on motocross tracks. Today, BMX bikes are also used to do tricks and jumps in freestyle events.

BMX racers go over jumps as they ride around a track.

F A C T !

The first BMX bikes were made with Schwinn Stingrays.

Mountain Bikes

The first mountain bikes were built in California in the late 1970s. Mountain bikes are larger than BMX bikes. They are built with light frames and fat tires. They also have many gears. Mountain bikes are meant for off-road riding.

Bicycles through the Years

Draisine

1817

Macmillan Bicycle

1839

Ordinary

1871

Lasting Popularity

After almost 200 years, the bicycle is still popular. Millions of bicycles are sold each year. In many countries, the bicycle is the best way to travel to work or school. Faster vehicles have been invented. But people still enjoy pedaling from place to place.

Elgin Original
1940

Schwinn 3-Speed
1970

Mountain Bike
2003

Fast Facts

- Around 1490, Leonardo da Vinci drew a picture of a machine similar to the first bicycle.

- Baron Karl Drais Von Sauerbrun built the first bicycle in 1817. It was called the *draisine*.

- In 1839, Kirkpatrick Macmillan made the first bicycle with pedals.

- The ordinary was invented in 1871. It had a large front wheel and a small back wheel.

- In 1885, John Starley built the first modern bicycle. It was called the Starley Rover.

- In 1888, John Boyd Dunlop introduced the first air-filled tires for a bicycle.

- The first mountain bikes were built in California in the late 1970s.

Hands On: Changing Gears

Most bicycles have gears to help people pedal on flat areas and hills. See how changing gears changes tire rotation. Ask an adult to help you with this activity.

What You Need

bicycle with gears   pencil

chalk   paper

What You Do

1. Turn the bicycle upside down so it rests on its seat and handlebars.
2. Shift the bicycle into the lowest gear. The chain will be on the smallest chain wheel and the back tire's largest gear.
3. Draw a small line at the top of the back tire with the chalk.
4. Slowly turn the bicycle's pedal in one complete circle. As the pedal turns, count how many times the chalk line goes around. Write the number of turns on a piece of paper.
5. Shift the bicycle into the highest gear. The chain will be on the largest chain wheel and the back tire's smallest gear.
6. Turn the back tire so the chalk line is at the top.
7. Slowly turn the bicycle's pedal so it makes one complete circle. Count how many times the chalk line goes around this time. Write the number of turns on your piece of paper.

The back tire should go around more times in a high gear than in a low gear. The low gear covers less ground with each turn of the pedals. The high gear covers more ground.

Glossary

calipers (KAL-uh-purz)—a set of clamps at the end of a brake cable that press against a wheel's rim to stop the wheel from turning

chain wheel (CHAYN WEEL)—a gear that moves a bicycle chain

crank (KRANGK)—a bar that is attached at a right angle to a chain wheel of a bicycle

derailleur (di-RAY-lur)—a device that moves a chain from one gear to another on a bicycle

freewheel (FREE-weel)—a set of five to nine gears on the back tire of a bicycle; the freewheel spins in one direction and locks in the other.

friction (FRIK-shuhn)—a force made when two objects rub together

gear (GEER)—a toothed wheel that fits into a bicycle chain

hydraulic (hye-DRAW-lik)—having to do with a system powered by fluid forced through pipes or chambers

Internet Sites

FactHound offers a safe, fun way to find Internet sites related to this book. All of the sites on FactHound have been researched by our staff.

Here's how:
1. Visit *www.facthound.com*
2. Type in this special code **0736826688** for age-appropriate sites. Or enter a search word related to this book for a more general search.
3. Click on the **Fetch It** button.

FactHound will fetch the best sites for you!

Read More

Beyer, Mark T. *Bicycles of the Past.* Transportation through the Ages. New York: PowerKids Press, 2002.

Deady, Kathleen W. *BMX Bikes.* Wild Rides! Mankato, Minn.: Capstone High-Interest Books, 2002.

Kelley, K. C. *Mountain Biking.* Extreme Sports. Milwaukee: Gareth Stevens, 2004.

Shuter, Jane. *Cycle Power: Two-Wheeled Travel Past and Present.* Travel through Time. Chicago: Raintree, 2004.

Index